STAB YOUR WAY TO THE TOP

ABOUT THE AUTHOR

Martin Wakeman's cartoons have appeared in many publications including, the **Mirror, The Sun,** and **Men Only**. By day he applies aggressive management in an I.T. department but will punch anyone on the nose if they call him a computer nerd.

STAB YOUR WAY TO THE TOP

Martin Wakeman

KOGAN
PAGE

YOURS TO HAVE AND TO HOLD
BUT NOT TO COPY

First published in 1995

Apart from any fair dealing for the purposes of research or private study, or criticism or review, as permitted under the Copyright, Designs and Patents Act, 1988, this publication may only be reproduced, stored or transmitted, in any form or by any means with the prior permission in writing of the publishers, or in the case of reprographic reproduction in accordance with the terms and licenses issued by the CLA. Enquiries concerning reproduction outside those terms should be sent to the publishers at the undermentioned address:

Kogan Page Limited
120 Pentonville Road
London N1 9JN

© Martin Wakeman, 1995

British Library Cataloguing in Publication Data

A CIP record for this book is available from the British Library.

ISBN 0 7494 1718 8

Typeset by BookEns Limited, nr Royston, Herts.
Printed and bound in Great Britain by Biddles Ltd, Guildford and Kings Lynn

WHAT IS AGGRESSIVE MANAGEMENT?

WHAT IS AGGRESSIVE MANAGEMENT?

Aggressive Management is the fear that some
managers can instil by their very presence.

WHAT IS AGGRESSIVE MANAGEMENT?

WHAT IS AGGRESSIVE MANAGEMENT?

It's the ability to inject adrenalin into subordinates.

WHAT IS AGGRESSIVE MANAGEMENT?

It's the ability to make people think that you are
bothered by what they do.

WHAT IS AGGRESSIVE MANAGEMENT?

It's the ability to make people feel uneasy about
your intentions.

WHAT IS AGGRESSIVE MANAGEMENT?

It's the ability to motivate people even when you're not there.

WHAT IS AGGRESSIVE MANAGEMENT?

It's the ability to let people know they're in the
wrong without even telling them.

WHAT IS AGGRESSIVE MANAGEMENT?

It's the ability to instil competition.

WHAT IS AGGRESSIVE MANAGEMENT?

It's the ability to get people to call you by your correct title.

WHAT IS AGGRESSIVE MANAGEMENT?

It's the ability to make everybody glad they're not in the wrong.

WHAT IS AGGRESSIVE MANAGEMENT?

It's the ability to make people realise that the workplace is for work.

WHAT IS AGGRESSIVE MANAGEMENT?

It's the ability to make people feel guilty even
when you're on holiday.

WHAT IS AGGRESSIVE MANAGEMENT?

It's the ability to make people feel guilty.

WHAT IS AGGRESSIVE MANAGEMENT?

It's the ability to make people scared to fail.

WHAT IS AGGRESSIVE MANAGEMENT?

It's the ability to make people WORK
for you.

How do we gain these skills?
We look at the people who succeed ...

THE PEOPLE WHO SUCCEED

THE PEOPLE WHO SUCCEED

There are two types of people who succeed in an organisation and get into good management positions.

Looking paradoxically at the empirical reasoning behind the total repurchasing mechanism ...

1. THE
CLEVER
PEOPLE

THE PEOPLE WHO SUCCEED

2. THE
NOT-SO-CLEVER
PEOPLE

THE PEOPLE WHO SUCCEED

Clever people get on because of their ability to understand business processes and being able to act on knowledge ahead of contemporaries.

Unfortunately most of us are not so clever!

Not-So-Clever people do not possess such intellectual reasoning and will have to rely on other techniques to succeed.

THE PEOPLE WHO SUCCEED

So most of the people who succeed have to use other techniques.

THE PEOPLE WHO SUCCEED

One of the key elements of Aggressive techniques is to get a 'Clever' person working for you.

THE PEOPLE WHO SUCCEED

Then use their cleverness ...

This is not so difficult as most clever people are not so bright.

THE PEOPLE WHO SUCCEED

So you don't have to be clever to succeed.

This can be illustrated by examining the people above you.

How many of them are cleverer than you? – not many I bet.

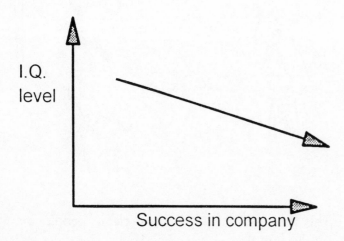

THE PEOPLE WHO SUCCEED

Note how people use simple terms to explain things to directors and chairmen. It's almost like talking to children.

The computer says that stock levels are very high. This means that we are holding very high levels of stock.

Sorry, can we take it a little slower? First of all: what's a computer?

THE PEOPLE WHO SUCCEED

SO ...

bosses may not be clever,

BUT They do hold the key to your career.

7 WAYS TO IMPRESS YOUR BOSS

With a little effort you should be able to convince
your boss that you are good managerial material.

7 WAYS TO IMPRESS YOUR BOSS

1. Never be afraid to tell superiors of your achievements.

7 WAYS TO IMPRESS YOUR BOSS

2. Never be afraid to tell superiors of their achievements.

7 WAYS TO IMPRESS YOUR BOSS

3. Never be afraid to be condescending and patronising about your staff;

but take the credit for their good work.

7 WAYS TO IMPRESS YOUR BOSS

4. Never be afraid to take credit for any joint activity.

7 WAYS TO IMPRESS YOUR BOSS

5. Never be afraid to pretend to have thought of things even before the person who really has the idea.

7 WAYS TO IMPRESS YOUR BOSS

7 WAYS TO IMPRESS YOUR BOSS

6. Never be afraid to find a way to create conversation 'hooks' for future meetings.

7 WAYS TO IMPRESS YOUR BOSS

7 WAYS TO IMPRESS YOUR BOSS

7. Never be afraid to run other people down,

subtly sowing the seeds of doubt.

NOBODY EVER GOT PROMOTED FOR DOING THEIR JOB WELL!

Remember this when trying to impress your boss:

You are *expected* to do the job well. So forget about normal duties and concentrate on doing things that are important to your career and not the company.

NOBODY EVER GOT PROMOTED FOR DOING THEIR JOB WELL!

Your company is in business to make a product or give a service. It is not in business to make you happy.

So look after number 1.

and distance yourself from failures!

NOBODY EVER GOT PROMOTED FOR DOING THEIR JOB WELL!

So how do we become 'Aggressive Managers'?

If you are a NICE person then you may need to act against your instinctive NICE behaviour. This is difficult ...

Dr Jeckyll

Mr Hyde

It is not instantaneous. It takes determination because it is not only your verbal communication that must be toughened up but your non-verbal signals too ...

AGGRESSIVE BODY LANGUAGE

AGGRESSIVE BODY LANGUAGE

If you are going to succeed in aggressive management then it is important to toughen up your non-verbal communications. Here are some tips on how to deal with meeting different people in the organisation

1. Dealing with a subordinate

Always phone them to come and see you and don't tell them why. They then have to interrupt whatever they are doing.

She wants to see me

They are already worried about whether or not they have done anything wrong.

AGGRESSIVE BODY LANGUAGE

When they arrive always be doing something else. On the phone or signing papers or anything to keep them waiting until you are ready to see them. In this way you emphasise that your time is more precious than theirs.

AGGRESSIVE BODY LANGUAGE

Keep eye contact and call them by their first name more than once during the conversation. Telling of names can be very unsettling.

Lean forwards for most of the discussion (but see page 49).

AGGRESSIVE BODY LANGUAGE

Pointing with finger or pen is very aggressive.

AGGRESSIVE BODY LANGUAGE

Lean forwards most of the time but don't be
afraid to lean back and appear to relax.

Make sure your visitor's chair doesn't tilt so they
cannot copy your more relaxed style.

AGGRESSIVE BODY LANGUAGE

The layout of your office is very important.

Your chair should be higher than theirs so you can look down on them.

Keep the desk between them and you symbolically protecting your groin and maintaining them and us position.

AGGRESSIVE BODY LANGUAGE

A separate meeting table is a good idea because you are leaving behind the weighty matters of high office to condescend to talk to the subordinate.

AGGRESSIVE BODY LANGUAGE

Never have much on your desk apart from a few files with headings such as 'Budget', 'Manpower Resources' or 'Strategy Papers', all marked with future dates indicating that you have access to the long-term view denied to the subordinate.

AGGRESSIVE BODY LANGUAGE

Getting your secretary to bring coffee is a good idea because it indicates to the subordinate that you can have such things delivered while he/she has to go to the vending machine.

NB Always have coffee in cups and saucers (never use a mug) even if the coffee originates from the same vending machine; get your secretary to transfer its contents to the cup.

AGGRESSIVE BODY LANGUAGE

If you want them to do some good work for you tell them you are relying on them to produce some good work and to produce it on time.

People's natural instinct is to try to protect the people who rely on them.

They will work harder in the hope that you will reward them.

Of course you won't ...

AGGRESSIVE BODY LANGUAGE

Make sure you end the discussion and are seen to
be getting on to the next item on your agenda.

AGGRESSIVE BODY LANGUAGE

2. Meeting with a superior

THE BIG CHEESE

If you can meet a superior in your office (in *your* territory) you have an immediate advantage but more often than not it will be on his/her territory.

AGGRESSIVE BODY LANGUAGE

Obviously if you are in their territory then their office will be laid out against you. So in order to redress the balance try these tricks:

Sit at an angle, if possible. Try to remove the restriction of the desk between you.

Notice and mirror the body movements of the superior. This subconsciously indicates agreement with his/her feelings and reasonings.

Take a file or folder or briefcase in with you. Not to open but to keep by your side. You immediately have somewhere else to go if things start to go wrong.

AGGRESSIVE BODY LANGUAGE

If possible try to adopt a superior position, for
example by coming round to their side of the
desk to show them something.

AGGRESSIVE BODY LANGUAGE

If you want them to believe you, open hands are
a sign of honesty.

Keep eye contact.

Don't go into a meeting unprepared.
Always jot down before hand (if possible)
what you want to say!

AGGRESSIVE BODY LANGUAGE

3. Peer to Peer contact

AGGRESSIVE BODY LANGUAGE

PEERS.

These people are your worst enemies.

Follow all the same procedures for superior contact but let the peer know that you are top dog!

Never phone yourself. Always get the secretary to make the call and connect you when the peer is waiting on the line. Make sure your secretary waits for four or five seconds before connecting you.

This snub will put your opponent on the defensive.

AGGRESSIVE BODY LANGUAGE

Always have somewhere else to go (real or imaginary) so that YOU terminate the meeting.

Stare at a spot just behind the other's ear. This is incredibly unsettling for the other person.

AGGRESSIVE BODY LANGUAGE

Remember you are always drawn to act in a way that boosts your self image. If you believe that the qualities of kindness and consideration are good and desirable then your non-verbal behaviour will attempt to react accordingly.

GET WISE

This is not a desirable way to act, to get on at work.

Nobody rewards the nice guy. People (and subordinates) may like you more but are more likely to walk all over you.

AGGRESSIVE BODY LANGUAGE

It is difficult to act out of nature. You can only change your personality over a period of time. It takes practice and determination to change both your verbal and non-verbal skills.

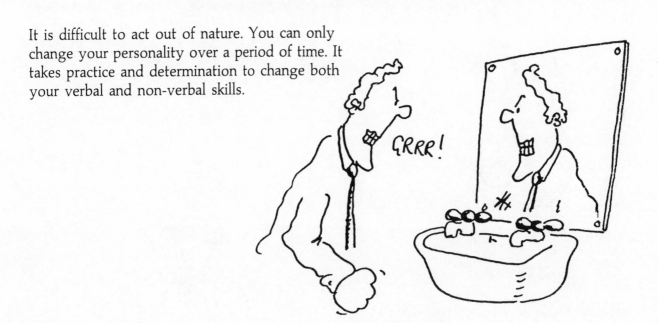

Use a mirror...

or practise on the dog.

HOW TO TREAT YOUR STAFF

HOW TO TREAT YOUR STAFF

Remember the old saying.

If you are going to eat an elephant ...

it's far easier if you force somebody else to do it for you.

HOW TO TREAT YOUR STAFF

Fortunately for the budding aggressive manager one of the strongest human instincts is that of a 'tribal' identity. One of the manifestations of this is that since you are their leader and representative your staff will stick by you and support you *no matter how you treat them.*

HOW TO TREAT YOUR STAFF

Your staff may hate you and call you rotten but
they will still defend you!

HOW TO TREAT YOUR STAFF

It is a natural instinct for people to want to please.
So the more difficult you are to please the harder
they will try.

KEEP YOUR STAFF ON EDGE

Lose your temper regularly ...

... but beware!

Never get angry and rant
unless you are sure of your ground and you know
you can win.

HOW TO TREAT YOUR STAFF

Pick on the weaker staff

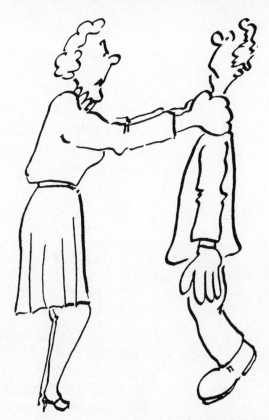

and introduce management by prejudice

HOW TO TREAT YOUR STAFF

It's good to have an individual you can pick on. It may be difficult for the individual but it's good for the rest of the staff to think ...

thank heaven it's him and not me!

HOW TO TREAT YOUR STAFF

Be angry, often, about the following. These are black and white issues about which you can be sure of your ground:

1. Not getting work finished on time
2. Bad timekeeping
3. People not working in works time

HOW TO TREAT YOUR STAFF

Introducing petty rules and restrictions really establishes your authority and is a cheap way of keeping your staff in line.

Some examples are:

1. Introduce a clear desk policy

A clear desk policy is a great technique because by insisting on tidiness you are acting in a mother substitute role and people respond instinctively.

HOW TO TREAT YOUR STAFF

Warn your staff that you are introducing a clear desk policy. Leave it for a week or so then one day after everyone has gone home collect up all the papers from people's desks and put them in your office so that they have to come to you to ask for them back.

HOW TO TREAT YOUR STAFF

2. Control the Mail

- Arrange for all mail to go through you.
- Insist that all mail leaving the department should come from you. (They write it, You sign it).
- Your secretary should open all incoming mail and have it ready for you at a certain time each day.
- Make little notes, underlines, highlights on the mail before sending it on to the relevant recipient.
- Ban the receipt of free trade newspapers and junk mail at work.

Free mail and papers are only free because of the adverts in it.

Adverts of alternative jobs for staff or services you probably don't need.

HOW TO TREAT YOUR STAFF

3. Decide that you must represent the group on all substantial committees

Ask for briefs from staff before going to these meetings. In this way they fulfil the Master-Slave relationship.

HOW TO TREAT YOUR STAFF

4. Restrict phone calls to local calls only

unless they need it for their job

HANDLING MEETINGS

HANDLING MEETINGS

Always speak first (or as near to the start as possible). This establishes you as the meeting's leader. Even if you didn't call the meeting.

This is especially relevant if you don't know much about the subject of a meeting. You can then outline the current situation and the problems to be resolved.

HANDLING MEETINGS

Next time you are in a meeting notice how the person who speaks first usually knows the least about the subject.

However don't think that's the end of your involvement.

Listen hard...

and butt in to state the obvious negative viewpoint.

But what about ...

In this way the others are always having to justify their theories to you, thereby continuing to emphasise your superiority.

HANDLING MEETINGS

Always make 'Action' notes on your own pad.

Say: 'If I can just review the agreed actions ...'
and proceed to list your notes.

Notice the word *agreed*

Make sure you don't get any actions

HANDLING MEETINGS

When you get back to your office ...

... give your secretary the actions to type up and circulate, making sure that other meeting members respond direct to you.

HANDLING MEETINGS

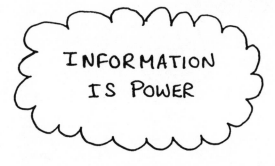

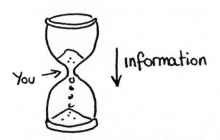

Keep the information flowing through you.

Keep vital information to yourself so only you can see the complete picture.

HANDLING MEETINGS

Sometimes a meeting can go on from morning to afternoon. This may involve a business lunch.

If it is possible **DON'T GO** ... unless there is somebody you want to make contact with over lunch.

Always have something 'more important' to do.

I have a briefing to prepare for the Chairman. Please excuse me.

There is nothing to be gained from idle chit-chat to subordinates, peers or immediate bosses.

They are then 'snubbed' and if your excuse is good they will feel left out of something important.

YOUR TEAM

YOUR TEAM

All people are different, however all teams or management groups have the same characters within them. If one of the group goes it is important to fill the gap with a 'like' character to get the right mix within the group.

A successful team will contain the right mix of the following characters:

 THE LEADER

 THE BRIGHT BASTARD

 THE DOER

 THE PARTY-GOER

 THE DULL BASTARD

 THE ORGANISER

 THE STRANGE BASTARD

YOUR TEAM

THE LEADER

You (hopefully)
co-ordinates the team. Does not need to be
brilliant or creative but will be the most assertive
and aggressive member of the group.

THE BRIGHT BASTARD

Introverted but intellectually dominant. The
source of most of the original ideas in the group.
Guard this man with your life.

YOUR TEAM

THE DOER

Takes the bright bastard's ideas and translates them into workable mechanisms. Gives them a start, finish and most often does the work as well. Nearly as important as the Bright Bastard but more difficult to spot.

THE PARTY GOER

Bright and cheerful, gregarious. Most popular member of the group. Can be a right pain in the neck but useful for WHO he knows.

YOUR TEAM

THE DULL BASTARD

Does the tasks allocated to him but will never have an original idea of his own.

THE ORGANISER

Makes sure everyone gets where they're supposed to. Makes sure all the typing is done, all expenses paid and is usually in charge of office stationery. In other words does all those jobs nobody else wants to do.

YOUR TEAM

THE STRANGE BASTARD

Usually belongs to some weird religious
organisation. Does not contribute much to the
team apart from giving everybody somebody
they can ridicule at office parties.

It is important that the team does not contain too
many of one sort. For example too many bright
bastards in your team will mean that they spend
all their time philosophically talking about the
problem and never getting the real work done.

Too many strange bastards and you might get a
morris dancing team.

SO TO SUM UP

Power is nice

so do what you can to GET it and KEEP it!

SO TO SUM UP

Treat your staff right

SO TO SUM UP

**Do unto your peers as they would do unto
you**

SO TO SUM UP

Make sure the bosses know who you are

SO TO SUM UP

But above all

make sure somebody else gets ALL the blame!!!

SO TO SUM UP

HAVE FUN but watch out for those other
aggressive buggers!

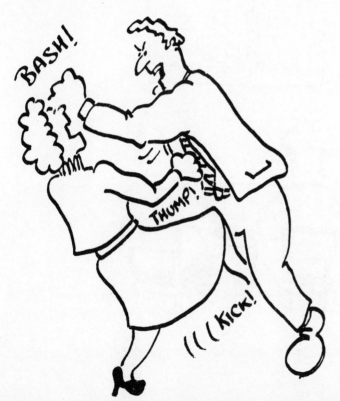

Because you won't get any
help or sympathy!!!